Robinson Public Library District
606 North Jefferson Street
Robinson, IL 62454-2699

Everything You Need to Know

# IF YOUR FAMILY IS ON WELFARE

Welfare can provide a temporary solution to families who are having trouble meeting their needs—food, shelter, clothing, and other necessities.

• THE NEED TO KNOW LIBRARY •

Everything You Need to Know

# IF YOUR FAMILY IS ON WELFARE

Arlene Erlbach

Robinson Public Library District
606 North Jefferson Street
Robinson, IL 62454-2699

THE ROSEN PUBLISHING GROUP, INC.
NEW YORK

Published in 1998 by The Rosen Publishing Group, Inc.
29 East 21st Street, New York, NY 10010

Copyright © 1998 by The Rosen Publishing Group, Inc.

All rights reserved. No part of this book may be reproduced in any form without permission in writing from the publisher, except by a reviewer.

First Edition

### Library of Congress Cataloging-in-Publication Data

Erlbach, Arlene.
   Everything you need to know if your family is on welfare / by Arlene Erlbach.
     p. cm.
   Includes bibliographical references and index.
   Summary: Provides basic information about the welfare system and dispels myths about welfare recipients.
     ISBN 0-8239-2433-5
   1. Aid to families with dependent children programs—United States—Juvenile literature. 2. Welfare recipients—United States—Juvenile literature. 3. Public welfare—United States—Juvenile literature.
[1. Public welfare.] I. Title.
HV699.E75   1996
362.7'13"0973—dc20                                      96-33395
                                                                                                        CIP
                                                                                                         AC

*Manufactured in the United States of America*

# Contents

| | |
|---|---|
| Introduction | 6 |
| 1. What Is Welfare? | 11 |
| 2. How It All Began | 17 |
| 3. How Did We Get Here? | 23 |
| 4. The Application Process | 31 |
| 5. Dealing with Your Emotions | 35 |
| 6. Difficult Situations | 43 |
| 7. Getting Back to Work | 48 |
| 8. Planning Your Future | 54 |
| Glossary—*Explaining New Words* | 58 |
| Where to Go for Help | 60 |
| For Further Reading | 62 |
| Index | 63 |

# Introduction

For as long as Carl can remember, his mom had managed the local town diner. Although the job was difficult for a single mother, it enabled her to support the two of them. Carl had spending money for movies, sports equipment, and fashionable clothes. But, about a year ago, the man who owned the diner passed away. His son sold the diner to a real estate developer, and it was torn down and an office building was put in its place. Carl's mom has not been able to find another job. All of the restaurants in the area require a college degree in restaurant management.

At first, Carl's mom received unemployment insurance. Once that ran out, Carl and his mom applied for welfare. Now they have barely enough money to pay for food and housing. Carl's mom is always very tense and worried about how the two of them will survive. Carl is embarrassed and angry when he doesn't have money to go out with his friends.

If your family's financial situation changes, you may have to go on welfare to meet your daily needs.

*However, things recently began to improve. The welfare caseworker told Carl's mom about some educational programs that can help her get a degree in restaurant management. She signed up for one of the programs and is attending classes. She should receive her degree in six months. With this degree, she should be able to get a job and get off welfare.*

Going on welfare is a scary experience. Changes may be happening at home and in your family which make it difficult to cope. Money will be tight. Food may be different or more scarce than before. There may be many interviews and applications that you and your parents will have to handle. Your parents may be embarrassed, angry, and impatient. With all of these changes, you will have questions and frustrations.

You may hear many stories about how only certain types of people go on welfare. You may also be told that once you go on welfare, you will never learn to support yourself. These are myths, and they are not true. People of all races and all ages receive welfare. You should not be made to feel poorly because your family's financial situation is different from that of your friends. There is no reason to feel ashamed.

If your family has been on welfare for a while, you may wonder if it is permanent. If your family has been on welfare a short time, you may wonder when things will go back to the way they were.

# Introduction

You may wonder if you'll end up on welfare yourself. If you are receiving welfare payments for a child of your own, you may wonder how to change your situation and make life better for you and your child.

This book will talk about some of the organizations available to help you and your family through this difficult time. It will also talk about who to call for welfare applications, how to apply, and what to expect. It will discuss many of your concerns and ways to cope. Learning how welfare works, and what you can do to help yourself, will make your situation easier.

Food stamps are one type of welfare program available to help families obtain sufficient food and maintain proper nutrition.

# Chapter 1
# What Is Welfare?

Welfare is the term used to describe the government-sponsored programs that provide people with necessary resources when they are having trouble supporting themselves. This support includes cash assistance, housing assistance, health benefits, and food.

More than 12 million people of all races and ethnic backgrounds currently receive welfare benefits in the United States.

On August 22, 1996, President Bill Clinton signed the Personal Responsibility and Work Opportunity Reconciliation Act. According to the Center on Social Welfare Policy and Law (CSWPL), this law will cut $55 billion from U.S. welfare programs from 1996 until 2002. These cuts primarily affect the Food Stamp Program (providing needy families with coupons which can be used to buy food) and benefits to legal immigrants (people who work and live in the United States but are not U.S. citizens).

The following is a list of the major welfare programs currently available to help families. While many other welfare programs do exist for people without children, they will not be discussed in this book. For more detailed information, contact your social worker or state government office.

## TANF (Temporary Assistance for Needy Families)

One of the biggest changes caused by the welfare reform is the elimination of Aid to Families with Dependent Children (AFDC), emergency assistance, and work programs. They have all been replaced with a block grant known as Temporary Assistance for Needy Families or TANF. TANF is one of the largest welfare programs.

Under AFDC laws, poor families with children were *guaranteed* cash assistance to help with their food, housing, and clothing needs. This is no longer the case. With the program's elimination, the federal government will no longer decide which families are eligible. It will instead give each state a sum of money called a block grant. The state will then decide its own eligibility requirements. This means that requirements may vary greatly from state to state. What qualifies you and your family for assistance in one state, may not qualify you in another.

# What Is Welfare?

However, the federal government did provide a few general guidelines that must be observed. The following are two of the restrictions placed on families receiving welfare benefits:

- Families may not receive welfare benefits for more than five years. However, individual states may shorten this period.
- Each adult in the household is required to work twenty hours each week. Both education and job training will fill this requirement. The hours of work required each week will increase from 1997 through 2002.

Each state is given the power to override these requirements in 20 percent of all cases if it can show good reason to do so. Also, because of the change in funding, it is possible that even if your family meets all of the eligibility requirements, you may still be placed on a waiting list to receive payments.

## Food Stamps

Food stamps are used in place of cash when buying food. They can help you and your family afford nutritious food. They are provided by the government to low-income people to ensure that they will have food.

Like other welfare benefits, your family must apply to receive food stamps. Both an application and interview are required before your case is processed. This interview will also qualify you for medical assistance if your family meets the requirements. The application is available from the local welfare or social services office.

Once the application is completed and sent to the social services office, the head of your household should call and schedule an interview with a social worker. The government will then inform you within thirty days if your food stamp application has been accepted or denied.

Be sure to tell the social worker if you are in an emergency (you have little or no income, or your other bills leave your family no money for food). In many states you can apply for Expedited Food Stamps. If you meet the requirements, you will be interviewed immediately and informed of the decision that day. The food stamps should arrive within five days if you qualify.

Once you have qualified for the Food Stamp Program, it is your responsibility to pick them up at an approved site. The pick-up sites in your area should be listed and included in your acceptance information. If not, the site listings are available through your local social services office.

## Medicaid

Medicaid provides help for people who cannot pay for their medical care. The benefits are available to any family who qualified for AFDC payments under the old welfare guidelines (before August 1,

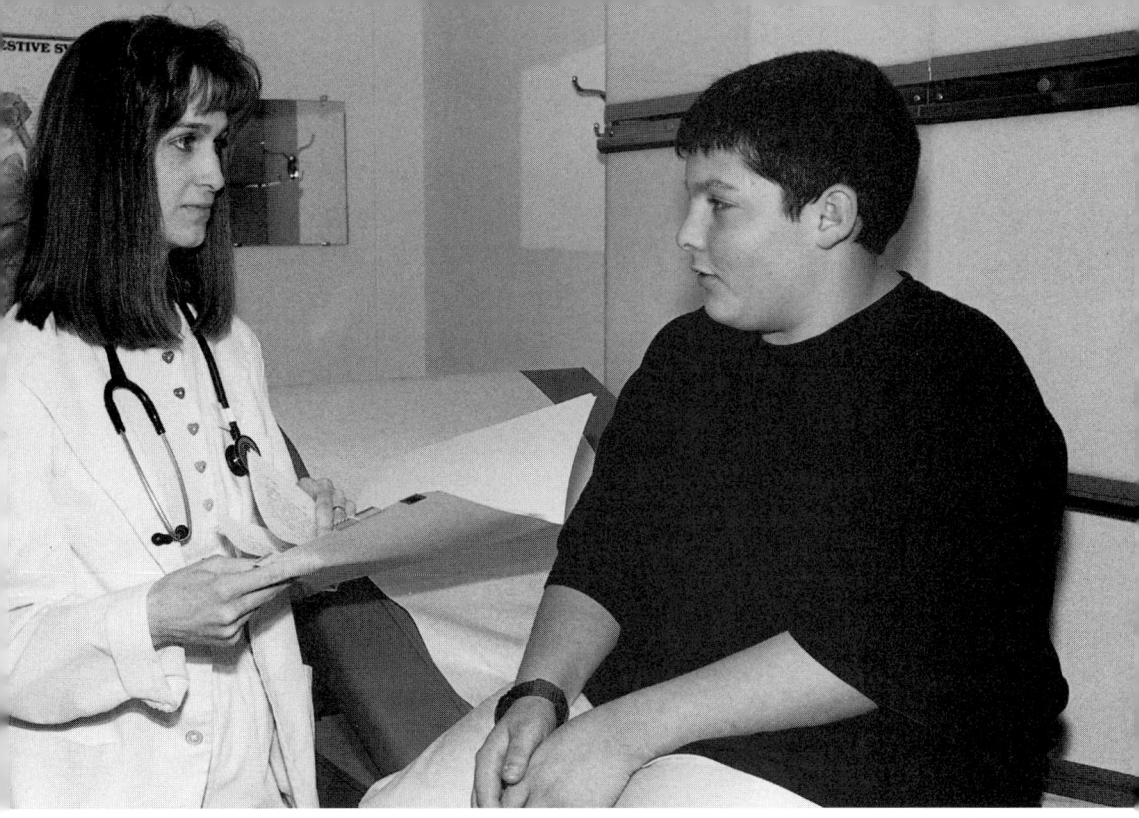

Welfare recipients can receive medical treatments and benefits through a program called Medicaid.

1996). If you are applying for TANF payments, you do not have to fill out a separate application for Medicaid.

Once your application is approved, you are entitled to free medical benefits. You will receive a Benefit Identification card. Show this card to the doctor, hospital, or drugstore when you receive treatment. Your bills will then be sent directly to the state. Not all places accept Medicaid, so be sure to check first.

Depending on your family's financial situation, you may be required to pay part of the medical costs. This is called a co-payment and it is expected at the time that you receive the medical care. The co-payment can range from 50¢ up to $25.00 and above.

If you are unable to afford the co-payment, tell the doctor, hospital, or drugstore. They cannot refuse you treatment or medicine because you are unable to provide the co-payment. If this should happen, call the Office of Medicaid Management at (800) 541-2831 to report the problem.

There may be a limit to the number of doctor visits and medicine for which Medicaid will pay. It is important to check with your social worker about the laws for your state.

## Housing Assistance

In some states your family may receive a rent subsidy. The Department of Public Aid will pay part of your rent, or help your family move into low-income housing. Ask your caseworker if it is available and how to qualify for it.

Welfare programs provide ways for people to help themselves and their families. They were designed to assist families in getting themselves out of difficult situations.

According to the CSWPL, most families received AFDC benefits for no more than two years at a time. Less than half of the families received benefits for more than three years. Most people leave the system and remain financially secure the rest of their lives.

# Chapter 2
# How It All Began

"Let me assert my firm belief that the only thing we have to fear is fear itself.... Our greatest primary task is to put people to work...."

U.S. President Franklin Delano Roosevelt (FDR) spoke these words at his first inaugural speech in the 1930s. He was elected president at a time when the United States was at the height of the Great Depression. The U.S. financial system had completely collapsed. Sixteen million workers were unemployed. People's spirits were low, and the American public was desperate for some hope.

FDR offered that hope. As governor of New York, he began many domestic programs aimed at helping people get back to work and achieve better lives.

In his presidential campaign, FDR continued his efforts to help people. He promised America a "New Deal" to improve the country's situation.

Within his first 100 days in office, he created and passed a large number of welfare programs. These programs provided immediate economic relief to businesses and agriculture. He then assembled numerous government agencies to provide emergency aid and employment. In 1935, he created both the Works Project Administration and the Social Security Act, providing for the unemployed, the children, and the elderly.

Three years later Congress passed the Wage and Hours Act, establishing a minimum wage and limiting the number of hours people were required to work. After FDR died in office, Vice President Harry Truman assumed the presidency post. He, too, was a firm supporter of the New Deal and continued pressing for many of FDR's domestic policies.

Then, in the early 1960s, President John F. Kennedy began his domestic program, calling it the "New Frontier." Upon his assassination, Vice President Lyndon B. Johnson took over.

In 1964, Johnson called for a national "War on Poverty," outlining a vast program of economic and social welfare legislation. The new programs included Medicaid, the Food Stamp Program, and housing assistance. He also supported a series of new child welfare programs including the Child Nutrition Act, the Head Start program, and the Foster Grandparent program.

As the programs increased, the number of people on welfare also increased. By 1975, the parents of more than 56 percent of children on welfare were either divorced or separated. Unable to support themselves and their children alone, many women had turned to the welfare system. Also, when unemployment rates rose in the 1980s, so did the number of families on welfare.

In 1988, in an effort to curb the rising welfare numbers, Congress passed the Family Support Act. Among other things, its new programs focused on sending welfare recipients into the workforce. It increased funding for education and for job training. A new program, Job Opportunities and Basic Skills (JOBS), was created to help with this training and education.

In his first term as president, Bill Clinton set out to "end welfare as we know it." In 1994, he signed a reform based upon the 1988 Family Support Act. This was called the Work and Responsibility Act. It increased the education and training programs, but set a two-year limit on benefits. After this time, welfare recipients were either forced to work or lose their benefits.

He continued focusing on getting welfare recipients back into the workforce with his new legislation, passed during the summer of 1996, which drastically changed the U.S. welfare system. Under the new guidelines, severe time limits are imposed, restricting the length of time a family may remain on welfare. Restrictions are also imposed upon unwed mothers under age eighteen,

On August 22, 1996, President Clinton signed a bill calling for the most significant changes in the welfare system since its inception more than sixty years ago.

immigrants, and families that continue to have children while they are on welfare.

These reforms are an attempt to maintain many of the welfare programs, while reducing the federal budget spending. For the first time since its creation sixty years ago, the federal guarantee of cash assistance to needy families has been removed.

Welfare can help people sustain themselves and their families through difficult times, such as job loss or divorce.

# Chapter 3

# How Did We Get Here?

There are many reasons why a family becomes unable to support its needs. Sometimes one parent becomes sick, passes away, or leaves the family. Other times a natural disaster may destroy a house, leaving a family homeless. A family will often seek welfare benefits if one or both parents have lost a job. Whatever the reason, these situations leave a family with very little resources: food, clothing, shelter. Welfare offers temporary assistance to help such a family through this difficult time.

## Job Loss

*Sara and her brother had always had a nice home, good clothes, and generous allowances. Sara's dad had earned a good salary working at a local auto factory. Because their mom stayed at home to take care of them, she had never learned any business skills. But life changed for Sara and her family when the factory began replacing workers with machines. Many people, including her father, were laid off. Her dad's unemployment payments lasted for almost a year, but he still could not find work during that time. There was nothing available. Soon the family had spent all of its savings. To meet expenses, Sara's family applied for welfare.*

Without a regular income, money becomes tight. Things that you once had, you may no longer be able to afford. Job loss happens for many reasons. The following are a few of the more common reasons:

**Layoff**

When the company your parent worked for can no longer afford to pay him or her, it may temporarily have to stop your parent's employment. This is called a layoff. The company may have gone out of business—or needed to cut back on its payroll. It may also have merged with another business causing a change in staff. There are many complicated reasons for layoffs but the end result is the loss of an income for your family.

**New Technology**

Sometimes new technology replaces workers. Jobs once done by people may now be completed by machines more quickly and cheaply, which could result in people losing jobs.

It is important to learn about the new technology in your field.

Other times the job market changes and skills become outdated. For example, companies are now using computers instead of typewriters and voicemail instead of receptionists. Many companies expect their employees to know about the Internet, and send e-mail instead of office memos. People unfamiliar with new technology usually have difficulty finding office work. They may need to go on welfare temporarily until they learn the skills they need.

**Disability**

Sometimes a parent loses his or her job because of a disability. A disability is a sickness or injury that prevents him or her from working. For example, a parent who normally lifts and unpacks boxes at work might qualify for welfare benefits if she has had a back injury. A person who is ill with complications from diseases like AIDS (acquired immune deficiency syndrome) or cancer may also qualify because he is unable to work and support his family. Without an income, he can use welfare payments to help meet the family's expenses.

## Single-Parent Families

*Janie, her brother, and her parents lived in a spacious, suburban home. Her father had a good job as the sales manager of a large printing company. Janie's family was financially secure. When Janie was twelve, her parents divorced. Janie's mother had to go back to school to update her work skills. At first her father paid child support, and that helped her mom meet their expenses. After a year, the payments started arriving late. Janie's mom had difficulty paying bills. When Janie's father left town, the payments stopped. Janie's mom had to sell the house, and they had to move. Eventually Janie's mother was forced to apply for welfare while she attended school.*

A large percentage of families receive welfare because a parent is absent from the home. In 1994, AFDC provided cash assistance to about 4.2 million single mothers and their children. There are many reasons that one parent is absent from

## Child Support

Parents are legally responsible for supporting their children. In cases where your parents do not live together, the court will define these responsibilities. It will grant one parent primary custody of the child(ren) and the other parent will be instructed in his or her financial obligations and visitation rights. These obligations are called child support. Based upon the non-custodial parent's wages and other income, debts, and expenses, the court will order a specific amount of child support to be paid regularly.

A parent who refuses to pay child support (once it is established by the court) is breaking the law. All states have programs that enforce child support payments.

There are many different methods that the state can use to ensure that the support payments are met. They include: reporting the late payments to credit bureaus and banks; removing the amount owed from the parent's paycheck; and arresting the parent for not obeying the laws of the court. Because some of these methods may require a fee, be sure to ask before taking any action.

For help with late child support payments, call the national child support help line (800) 228-KIDS.

Talking with a family member, friend, or counselor may help you through some of your frustrations and extra stress.

the home. The parents may be divorced or separated. They may have never married, and have little or no contact with each other. One parent may have abandoned the family and be unable, or unwilling, to pay child support even if it is required by law. Whatever the reason, it is very difficult to support a family on one income.

## Low-Income Jobs

Families sometimes need to apply for welfare benefits even if one parent is working. Some jobs do not pay a high enough salary to meet a family's expenses; other jobs are only part-time. TANF payments will help the family pay their bills until one or both parents can get a better paying job, or until some bills are paid.

This is a difficult time for both you and your parents. To deal with this extra stress, it may help for you to discuss your feelings with your family. Tell them about your concerns and frustrations. If your family is uncomfortable with this, talk with a relative. There are no right or wrong feelings. If someone is uncomfortable talking, it is better not to pressure them with questions. Remember that everyone is experiencing many different emotions, and coping to the best of his or her ability.

In order to receive welfare benefits, your parent is required to fill out a detailed application.

# Chapter 4
# The Application Process

Applying for welfare can be an upsetting process. It may feel like the last in a series of financial troubles. You may believe that you or your family has failed to live up to certain expectations. But difficult situations happen to everyone. There is no need to feel embarrassed or ashamed.

According to the CSWPL, 9.5 million children in 5 million families received public aid payments between October 1992 and September 1993.

The first step in the welfare application process is to call or visit your local welfare office and request an application package. The phone number for the welfare office will usually be printed under the *State Government Listings* or *Community Service Numbers* in the White Pages of your phone book. It may be listed alphabetically under names such as:

The interview may be difficult, and at times embarrassing. However, it is a necessary part of the process.

- Department of Children and Family Services
- Department of Public Aid
- Department of Social Services
- Welfare Department

A family's eligibility for welfare depends on federal and state rules. It also depends on your family's assets (money and possessions) and any other sources of income.

The welfare application is long and contains many personal questions. This is a legal document, and the applicant has a responsibility to answer all questions completely and honestly. Here are some examples of questions that might appear on the application:

# The Application Process

- Do you have any savings?
- Do you own your home or rent?
- When have you last lived with your spouse?

Once the application is filled out and returned, the parent or caregiver of the children must schedule a face-to-face interview with a welfare caseworker. If you need assistance for yourself, or your own child, you must be present at the interview. Be prepared to answer questions about the following:

- your education, training, and work history
- job skills
- child care needs

At the interview the caseworker will ask you to prove many things. These include: your identity, your age, your address, your expenses, your income, and your resources (i.e. bank accounts, life insurance, real estate). The caseworker will also ask you about your job skills and experience. He or she will talk with you about any education or training you may need in order to get a job.

## When Will Welfare Payments Begin?

It may take a month or more for your family to receive payments. Once you are informed that you have qualified, there will be a local issuance site (place where welfare payments are distributed) listed in the paperwork. You will also receive a Benefit Identification card. You will need this card to pick up your benefits. Pick-up dates will be listed on your paperwork. It is important that you pick up the benefits promptly.

Be sure to tell your caseworker if your family is in immediate need of funds. He or she should also help you find shelter if your family has become homeless. It is important that you or your parent discuss with your caseworker any problems that you may have. Even if the caseworker seems rushed, it his or her responsibility to answer all of your questions.

# Chapter 5
# Dealing with Your Emotions

Not having money for the things that you want and need is very stressful. You and your family may feel angry or depressed, but you are not alone. Many families—both on and off welfare—experience these same frustrations.

*Rosa's class was taking a field trip to the Art Museum. Each student needed to pay $5 for the entrance fee and bring a lunch from home. Rosa really wanted to go on the trip, but she was concerned about talking to her mother. For the past year, Rosa's family has been on welfare. Her parents were divorced. When her father remarried, he stopped paying child support. Rosa's mother had recently been laid off, and she was having trouble finding new work.*

*When Rosa gave her mom the permission slip, her mother became angry. She yelled at Rosa for being selfish.*

*"Who's supposed to pay for this trip?" she screamed. Rosa left the room crying. Later she and her mom talked about what had happened. Rosa's mom apologized for screaming. She explained to Rosa how the money for the field trip was now a major expense. She was frustrated that she didn't have the money to give to Rosa. Rosa and her mother agreed to try and be more understanding toward each other and work together as a family.*

Welfare payments are often very small. According to the CSWPL, 52 percent of families receiving both TANF payments and food stamps during 1993 were left in poverty. Welfare benefits alone are not enough to support most needy families. Because of this, life on welfare is very stressful.

Let's look at a welfare family's budget in Illinois. The welfare benefits offered in Illinois are about average when compared with other states in the nation. A family of four receives TANF payments of about $414 each month. This money must be used for rent, utilities, clothing, and any household and school expenses.

The value of the food stamps the family receives would total $400 each month. But the food stamps cannot be used for any nonfood items, such as

# Dealing with Your Emotions

soap, toilet paper, or toothpaste. If the family's only income is from TANF, and its rent is $300 a month, this only leaves $114 to pay for utilities and other nonfood necessities—or about $3.80 per day for the entire family.

Having such limited resources emotionally affects a family. Here are some of the emotions your family may experience when living on welfare.

## Stress

Living on a tight budget is stressful for everyone involved. It can make a person feel pressured or tense.

When money becomes scarce, a family will have to go through some changes. These changes may be upsetting for both you and your family. Your parents may feel overwhelmed with the new financial responsibilities. If your parent has lost a job, he or she may feel guilty or depressed. If forced to accept a lower-paying job, your parent may feel ashamed and disappointed that he or she let you down.

No matter what the reason, these feelings create extra stress. You can help relieve this stress by being supportive at home. Offer to help with household chores or watch younger siblings while your parents look for a new job.

If you are on welfare because *you* have become a parent yourself, you may feel uncomfortable with the new responsibilities. You may have mixed

It may be difficult to deal with the many changes—both emotional and financial—that your family will experience on welfare. A counselor can often help you work through some of your feelings.

# Dealing with Your Emotions

feelings about the baby's other parent. He or she may or may not want to become involved with the child. However, the other parent is required by law to help you support your child. If he or she is unwilling, be sure to speak with your caseworker.

Check with your caseworker to see if you can receive counseling to help you deal with your emotions. You can also discuss your situation with your school counselor or social worker.

## Embarrassment

In some situations you may feel embarrassed about being on welfare. You may not be able to buy the trendiest clothing or afford to go out with your friends as often. This may make you feel uncomfortable around your friends. However, your true friends hopefully will be understanding and supportive through this time.

Know that everyone goes through difficulties in their lives. A great way to handle these periods is to work towards changing the situation.

## Resentment/Anger

You may feel angry with your parents for not being able to support you on their own. You may be resentful at having to accept welfare payments. These are all normal feelings. You may want to yell at your parents, but this will not improve the situation.

If you are receiving welfare payments for a child of your own, you may feel angry toward your child or his or her other parent. You may become so angry that you want to yell, but this also won't help the situation. It will only make you angrier with yourself—and you may end up hurting your child. If you feel that you are having trouble controlling your anger, speak to a counselor or somebody you trust. He or she will help you find better ways to deal with your feelings.

## Depression

When someone is depressed, he or she feels sad and may become withdrawn. There are many different ways that a depressed person may act. They may frequently cry or may seem to have no energy to do anything. They may sleep or watch the television for many hours. When these things do not make them feel better, they may become even more depressed.

If either you or your parents feel this way for a long time, you should contact your caseworker. He or she will be able to give you the names of organizations where you or your family can get help from a counselor or social worker, free of charge.

There are also free hot lines that you may call to seek advice and counseling. A number of these are listed in the back of this book. A counselor or social worker can help the depressed person cope with his or her feelings of sadness.

# Illegal Temptations

When money is tight, illegal activities may seem like an easy way to get money or escape your problems. But getting involved in things like shoplifting, drugs, and prostitution is not the answer. These crimes could lead to an arrest, criminal record, and possible jail sentence. With a criminal record, it is very difficult to obtain a job.

## Drug or Alcohol Abuse

Sometimes you may be tempted to try illegal drugs, such as marijuana, crack, cocaine, heroin, or LSD. You may consider drinking alcohol. These drugs may temporarily help you forget your situation, but they will not solve your problems. When the high wears off, your problems are still there.

Taking these drugs can lead to an addiction that will be costly and difficult to break. Drugs are also dangerous and illegal.

## Joining Gangs

You may be tempted to join a gang, particularly if your family has recently moved to a new neighborhood. Most gangs expect members to follow certain rules. Some may expect you to deal drugs, steal, or murder. While no one wants to be alone, there are many other ways to belong. If you are in a situation where you need to make new friends, contact a local religious or community center. Join clubs at school and get involved in activities that interest you.

## Counseling

It can be difficult to cope with the changes that your family is experiencing. You may have questions about your family's new situation. You may want to find out better ways to deal with the changes you are experiencing. Local clergy and school counselors are a good place to begin finding answers. If they cannot help you, they can give you the names of agencies that can. These people will listen and help you find ways to cope.

# Chapter 6
# Difficult Situations

When a family must live on welfare, it will have to make some big changes. If this happens to your family, you may feel angry. Trying to live within a small budget can make a person feel frustrated and alone. But understanding these new situations can help you learn to deal with them.

## Lack of Food

Sometimes a family will run out of food stamps before the end of the month. This may force you to change your eating habits. The food you like may no longer be available—or your family may run out of food. Local food pantries provide food to needy families to keep them from being hungry. The number for Second Harvest, a national service, is provided in the Where to Go for Help list in the back of this book.

It may be difficult and frightening if your family cannot pay all of its bills each month. But there are many organizations available to help you find a solution.

## Lack of Utilities

Sometimes your family may not have enough money to pay for utilities. Utilities are things like heat, electricity, or telephone service.

If it is very cold and your heat is turned off, call your local utility company. Talk to someone there to see if there are any payment options that will work within your family's budget. In some states it is illegal for the utility company to turn off your heat even if you can't pay the bill. It is best to contact your local welfare office, legal aide, or community center for help.

# Difficult Situations

You can conserve electricity by using lights only when you need them, and limiting the time you use your television or stereo. If the electricity to your home is turned off because your family is unable to pay the bill, your caseworker will help your parents contact organizations that can help.

The phone is necessary for reaching help. If your family is unable to afford one, or unable to pay the phone bill, find out where the pay phones are in your area. However, it is important to know that the emergency phone number, 911, will always reach the police—even if your phone service has been disconnected.

Some states offer programs that can help families with the cost of utilities. One of these, the Home Energy Assistance Program, provides assistance with utility bills and repairs. Discount telephone services may also be available. Contact your local telephone company to find out if it offers lower rates to families receiving public aid.

## Moving

If your family goes on welfare, you may need to move. Your parents may no longer be able to afford the rent or mortgage payments for your present home. You may have to move to a smaller house, or a cheaper apartment.

Sometimes welfare recipients live in neighborhoods that become gentrified. This is when middle-income people move in and renovate low-

You may experience many changes in your life. The things you took for granted, such as the telephone, may become unaffordable luxuries.

income areas, causing higher rents. If this happens in your neighborhood, your family may have a difficult time paying the higher rent and may have to move.

If your family has to move, try to visit the new neighborhood before the move. Find out about activities in the area. Try to visit your new school. After the move, keep in touch with your old friends. Call, visit them, or invite them to see you. It is important, especially at this time, to keep a connection with your old life. Do your best to make new friends, join new activities, and attempt to get involved in the new neighborhood.

# Difficult Situations

## Getting Evicted

If your family is unable to pay the rent or mortgage, you may receive an eviction notice. This is an official document—given by the owner of the property—that forces you to leave your home if you fail to pay the rent or mortgage. If it seems like eviction is a possibility for your family, call your welfare caseworker. He or she will inform you of your options.

## Homelessness

Homelessness is a growing problem. Low-income housing is rare, and people are sometimes unable to find a new home. These people often have no place to go and are forced to live on the streets. Call your welfare office if you feel that your family is in danger of losing your home. They may be able to help you find temporary shelter for your family.

When your family is on welfare, it is important to realize that the situation will not last forever. By working together, your family can overcome its financial struggles.

# Chapter 7

# Getting Back to Work

Getting back to work, or getting a better-paying job, is the first step to getting off of welfare. This often seems like an overwhelming responsibility. Many people feel that they don't know how to go about looking for a job. Other people feel that they lack the education to get a higher-paying job. It can also be frightening to think about losing the regular welfare payments, the food stamps, and Medicaid.

But getting back to work is the only way to get yourself off of welfare. It will feel good to know that your family can financially support itself.

## Job Training

Every state has a job training program for welfare recipients. Many of these are offered by community colleges. Some companies also offer special training programs for employees on welfare. These programs help people learn the

# Getting Back to Work

skills they need to become employable or work better at the jobs they have. Forty-seven percent of welfare families stopped receiving benefits when the parent began a new job (CSWPL).

Many states offer special programs for young parents. If you do not have a high school diploma, you may be expected to return to school before entering into the training program. Check with your local welfare office to obtain the guidelines for your state.

Your welfare worker will give you or your parent(s) the details of each state's job training program. The counselor will also assess each participant's interests and goals. This helps him or her determine the best type of training.

The counselor is responsible for providing information about financial assistance for tuition. Some states will pay for child care and transportation while welfare recipients receive job training.

## Schooling Is Now the Job

Once a welfare recipient is accepted into a training program, the training becomes his or her "job." It is important for participants to take the training seriously. Certain guidelines must be followed. Some of the guidelines include:

- showing up for training regularly
- being on time for classes
- doing passable work

The new welfare legislation requires parents to work a certain number of hours each week. This work can include job training, community service programs, and high school education.

Breaking these rules may result in the participant's loss of both the training and his or her other welfare benefits.

## Initial Employment Assistance

Sometimes finding a job will require paying for transportation, uniforms, equipment, and child care. Some states offer these items free to people who qualify. It is important for welfare recipients to ask their caseworkers if these benefits are available. Once these items are provided, looking for a job becomes much easier.

## Workfare

Programs like Workfare or Work Pays permit a person on welfare to receive a reduced payment while he earns money from a job. In states that offer Workfare or Work Pays programs, the recipient's welfare payment is reduced $1 for every $3 he or she earns from an outside job. For example, assume your family receives a welfare check for $377 a month. If you or your parent has a job that pays $600 a month, the welfare check will be reduced by $200. You would now receive $177 per month from welfare. With the additional money earned from employment, you or your family would receive a total of $777 per month. That is more than twice the money received from welfare alone!

## Earned Income Tax Credit

Federal and state taxes take a large portion of each person's salary. This money adds up quickly, especially if you are on a tight budget. If your parents have dependents (children under the age of eighteen), or if you are a parent, you may be eligible for a program that will help reduce the amount of tax taken by the government. It is called Earned Income Tax Credit. The tax credit allows people with low-paying jobs to pay less taxes—and receive more money in each paycheck.

The amount of this tax break varies from state to state. The maximum credit for 1996 was $2,152

Through a part-time job, you can learn many useful skills, such as accounting and how to deal with people.

for a family with one child and $3,556 for a family with two or more children. Welfare payments do not count as money earned. Contact your welfare caseworker, social worker, or local tax office to get information for your state.

## Things You Can Do to Help

If you are a full-time student under eighteen years old and are not receiving welfare payments for a child of your own, you can help your family by getting a part-time job. Your salary will not be counted as part of your family's income.

Try to find a job that allows you to use the skills you may already have, such as typing, house paint-

# Getting Back to Work

ing, or car repair. If you work as a server in a restaurant or a delivery person, you may receive tips (extra money given by the customer in response for good service). You will learn new skills and gain valuable work experience. You will also be taking steps to prepare yourself for your future.

Some schools offer work study programs. You may earn money and receive credit while you work. Other schools may help you find part-time work. You can find out about these programs by checking at your school's guidance office.

Today many states have introduced programs that try to make it easier for people receiving welfare payments to begin supporting themselves with jobs.

# Chapter 8

# Planning Your Future

*Each day Keesha proudly puts on her nurse's uniform and drives to the local children's hospital. She knows the value of a job. Keesha was young when her mother died. Keesha's father was left to raise her by himself. Because he was disabled, the family lived on welfare payments.*

*While she was in school, Keesha worked hard and received high grades in science. She also enjoyed helping other people. Her school counselor suggested that she might try nursing school. Keesha was eligible for grants and loans that paid for her training. With her schooling she was able to receive a well-paying job. Her salary has allowed her to move into a new apartment complex with many other young professionals. Keesha is glad she spent time studying in both high school and college.*

Just because your parents have been on welfare does not mean that you will end up there. Only about 10 percent of children who grew up receiving welfare end up on welfare themselves. While there are no guarantees that you will not need welfare assistance in the future, there are many ways to help avoid it.

## Delaying Childbearing

If you are an unmarried woman with children, your chances of needing welfare increase greatly. Most of the adults receiving TANF are female, single parents, according to the CSWPL. Caring for a child makes it difficult to finish school and prepare for a job. Furthermore, if you do have a job, child care is very expensive.

Life is very difficult for single mothers and fathers. So it is wise to delay childbearing until you get your education and are emotionally ready to raise a child. If you are sexually active, you should use reliable birth control to avoid unplanned pregnancies.

## Staying in School

Graduating from high school is important. With an education, you have a better chance to learn skills that will help you obtain a steady job. According to the CSWPL, a family headed by a woman without a high school degree is almost three times as likely to end up on welfare as is a family headed by a woman who is a high school graduate. While some educated people do end up

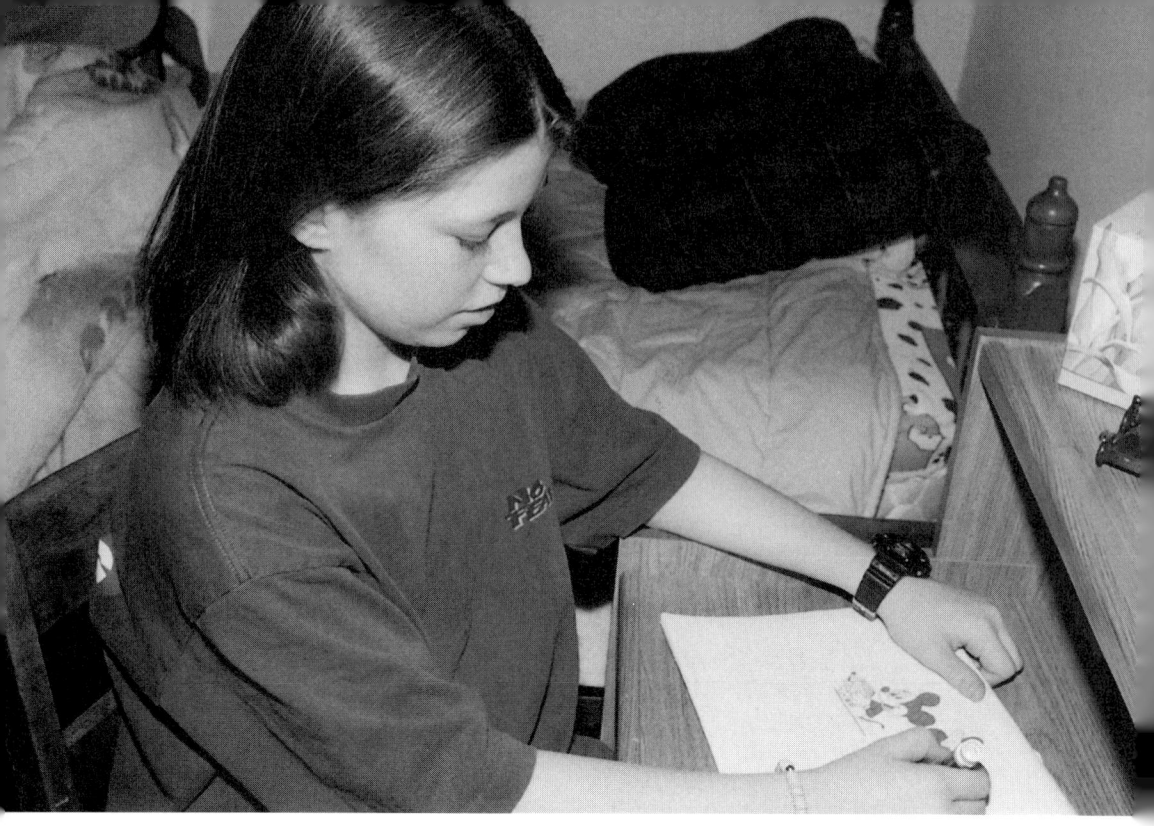

Developing your talents while in school can lead to a rewarding career.

on welfare, almost 70 percent of long-term welfare recipients did not graduate from high school.

Some high schools offer classes that will prepare you for a job. You may also want to go beyond high school for further training. More jobs, and better-paying ones, are available to people with higher educations usually from vocational schools or two-year or four-year colleges.

## Developing Talents and Interests

It is important to discover your talents and interests. Many of these can be developed into job skills. Examples include the ability to repair things

# Planning Your Future

easily or to work with children, or artistic skills. Maybe you like to play with animals, decorate, help your friends choose clothing, or do their hair.

Ask your school counselor how some of these interests and skills can lead you to a job in the future. He or she will tell you what training you will need. Your counselor may also know of ways you can use your skills at a job. Or maybe you can find ways to volunteer your skills, and use this to gain experience or meet other people who can help you get a future job.

## Taking Advantage of Advice

Your school counselor can help advise you on a career. He or she can look over your grades and your interests, and give you tests that can help you identify your talents. This may give you an idea of what you would like to do in the future.

Some companies offer part-time opportunities for high school students. They may hire these people full-time after they graduate. College aid programs are also available for students unable to afford a higher education. Check with your school counselor. He or she should know about them.

By making plans while you are in school, you are taking the first and most important steps to becoming employable. These steps may help you avoid becoming part of the welfare system in the future.

# Glossary—*Explaining New Words*

**abandon**  To take away protection or support.

**abuse**  The use of physical or verbal force to gain power over another person.

**assets**  Items that a family owns, such as a home, car, or bank account.

**child support**  The required payments provided by the noncustodial parent to the custodial parent for the financial support of the child.

**custodial parent**  The parent with whom the child lives.

**depression**  A continual feeling of hopelessness or sadness.

**disability**  The inability to perform a job due to an illness or injury.

**evict**  To be forced to leave your home by the bank or owner of the property.

**food stamps**  Coupons provided by the government that can be used to purchase food.

**grant**  The aid given to an individual for educational purposes.

**income**  Money earned by a person or household.

**layoff**  Loss of job, often temporarily, because of an employer's inability to afford the current number of employees.

**motivation**  The desire that causes a person to act or react.

# Glossary

**needy** The inability to obtain the necessities of life, such as food, clothing, and shelter, because of a lack of financial resources.

**rent subsidy** Money given by a state to welfare recipients to help pay their rent.

**repossess** To take back goods from a person because he or she has failed to make the required payments.

**TANF (Temporary Assistance for Needy Families)** Government-sponsored welfare block grant that provides money to each state for allocation to various welfare programs for families. This replaced AFDC, removing the federal guarantee of cash assistance to needy families.

**unemployment insurance** Payments made by the government to an individual when he or she is laid off. These payments are made regularly and for a specified amount of time.

# Where to Go for Help

**Boys Town National Hot Line**
(800) 448-3000

**Center on Social Welfare Policy and Law**
275 Seventh Avenue, 12th Floor
New York, NY 10001-6708
(212) 633-6967 / fax: (212) 633-6371
e-mail: HN0135@handsnet.org

**Information and Problem Resolution Unit**
c/o Department of Social Services
Hartford, CT 06106
(800) 228-KIDS

**National Center for Youth Law**
114 Sansome Street, Suite 900
San Francisco, CA 94194
(415) 543-3307 / fax: (415) 956-9024

**National Clearinghouse for Alcohol & Drug Abuse**
P.O. Box 2345
Rockville, MD 20847-2345
(800) 729-6686

**Parents Anonymous**
(909) 621-6184

**Second Harvest**
116 South Michigan Avenue
Chicago, IL 60603
(800) 771-2303 / fax: (312) 263-5626

# Where to Go for Help

**Single Parent Resource Center**
31 East 28th Street, 2nd floor
New York, NY 10016
(212) 951-7030 / fax: (212) 951-7037

**Teen Challenge**
444 Clinton Avenue
Brooklyn, NY 11238
(800) 501-1825 / fax: (718) 789-1439

**Women Work**
(800) 235-2732

# For Further Reading

Hammerslough, Jane. *Everything You Need to Know About Teen Motherhood.* Rev. ed. New York: The Rosen Publishing Group, 1997.

LeVert, Marianne. *The Welfare System: Help or Hindrance to the Poor?* Brookfield, CT: Millbrook Press, 1995.

Pollock, Sudie. *Will the Dollars Stretch? Teen Parents Living on Their Own.* Buena Park, CA: Morning Glory Press, 1997.

St. Pierre, Stephanie. *Everything You Need to Know When a Parent Is Out of Work.* New York: The Rosen Publishing Group, 1993.

Weiss, Ann E. *Welfare: Helping Hand or Trap?* Hillside, NJ: Enslow Publishers, 1990.

# Index

## A
Aid to Families with Dependent Children (AFDC), 12, 14, 16, 26
alcohol abuse, 41

## B
Benefit Identification card, 15, 34

## C
cash assistance, 11–12, 21
Child Nutrition Act, 18
child support, 26–28, 39
Clinton, President Bill, 11, 19
counseling, 42, 57

## D
Department of Public Aid, 16, 32
depression, 35, 37, 40
disability, 25–26, 54
divorce, 19, 26–28
drug abuse, 41

## E
Earned Income Tax Credit, 51–52
education, 13, 19, 33
embarrassment, 39
emergency assistance, 12, 14
emotions, dealing with, 35–42
employment assistance, 50
eviction, 47
Expedited Food Stamps, 14

## F
Family Support Act (1988), 19
food
    assistance, 11, 13–14
    lack of, 43
    stamps, 11, 13–14, 18, 36, 43, 48
Foster Grandparent program, 18

## G
gangs, 41–42
gentrification, 45–46

## H
Head Start, 18
health benefits, 11, 14–16
Home Energy Assistance Program, 45
homelessness, 23, 34, 47
hot lines, 40
housing assistance, 11, 16, 18

## I
Illinois, 36
immigrants, 11–12

## J
Job Opportunities and Basic Skills (JOBS), 19
job training, 13, 19, 33, 48–49
Johnson, Vice President Lyndon B., 18

## K
Kennedy, President John F., 18

## L
layoffs, 24, 35
low-income jobs, 28–29

## M
Medicaid, 14–16, 18, 48
minimum wage, 18
moving, 45–47

## N
New Deal, 18
New Frontier, 18
New York, 17

*63*

## P

Personal Responsibility and Work Opportunity Reconciliation Act, 11
poverty, 36

## R

resentment/anger, 39–40
Roosevelt, Franklin Delano (FDR), 17–18

## S

school, 49–50, 55–56
Second Harvest, 43
single mothers, 6, 19, 26–28, 55
single-parent households, 19, 23, 26–28
Social Security Act, 18
social workers, 14
stress, 36, 37–39

## T

Temporary Assistance for Needy Families (TANF), 12–13, 28–29, 36–37, 55
Truman, Vice President Harry S, 18

## U

unemployment, 17, 19, 23–24
insurance, 6, 24
United States, 11, 17
utilities, 37
lack of, 44–45

## W

Wage and Hours Act, 18
"War on Poverty," 18
welfare
application for, 13–15, 31–34
caseworkers, 33–34, 39, 40, 50
changes it brings, 8–9, 37, 43–47
description of, 11–16
example of payments, 36–37
getting off assistance, 48–53
history of, 17–21
interviews for, 13–14, 33
programs for children, 18–19
reforms, 11–13, 19–21
restrictions, 13, 19–21
who receives it, 8, 11, 31, 55
why it's needed, 23–29
Work and Responsibility Act (1994), 19
Workfare program, 51
Work Pays program, 51
work programs, 12
Works Project Administration, 18

## About the Author

Arlene Erlbach has written more than a dozen books for young people. Her young adult novel *Does Your Nose Get in the Way Too?* won an RWA Golden Medallion for best young adult novel. Its sequel, *Drop Out Blues*, was a semi-finalist the following year. She teaches elementary school in a Chicago suburb where she lives with her husband and teenage son.

## Photo Credits

Cover photo by Michael Brandt; photograph on page 20 by AP/Wide World; all other photos by Rita Rivera.